SIMPLE SLOW COOKER MEALS

~ 120 TASTY RECIPES ~

BARBOUR
PUBLISHING

Inspiration at your fingertips!

Looking for a simple way to bring new life to your kitchen? This book is for you. Within these pages, you'll find dozens of tasty recipes that are easy to prepare and are a delight to share with family and friends.

Finding a recipe is as easy as flipping through the book. At the bottom of each page, you'll see a color that corresponds to one of five categories:

EVERYDAY MEALS

CHILIES & STEWS

SEAFOOD SUPPERS

VEGGIE CASSEROLES & SIDES

DESSERTS & BEVERAGES

So set up this little book on your countertop, flip page after page for new culinary inspiration and kitchen tips and tricks, and you might just find a little encouragement for your soul in the process. Enjoy!

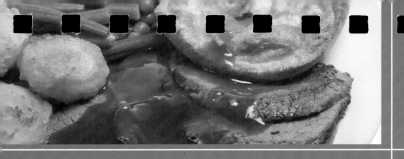

EVERYDAY MEALS

Everything God created is good, and to be received with thanks.
1 TIMOTHY 4:4 MSG

ITALIAN BEEF

1 (4 pound) rump roast
1 (14 ounce) can of beef broth
1 (8 ounce) jar of sliced pepperoncinis, undrained
1 (2 ounce) envelope dried Italian salad dressing mix

Combine all ingredients in slow cooker and cook on low for 8 to 10 hours until beef is tender and easy to shred. Serve in sandwiches topped with provolone cheese.

LEMON POT ROAST

2½ pounds chuck roast
1½ cups water
½ cup lemon juice
1 sweet onion, chopped
½ teaspoon salt
1 teaspoon celery salt
1 teaspoon onion salt
¼ teaspoon black pepper
¼ teaspoon marjoram
1 clove garlic, crushed

Put roast in shallow pan. Combine remaining ingredients in bowl and pour over roast. Cover and refrigerate overnight. Remove roast from marinade and place in slow cooker. Cover and cook on low 8 to 10 hours.

HANDY CONVERSIONS

1 teaspoon = 5 milliliters
1 tablespoon = 15 milliliters
1 fluid ounce = 30 milliliters
1 cup = 250 milliliters
1 pint = 2 cups (or 16 fluid ounces)
1 quart = 4 cups (or 2 pints or 32 fluid ounces)
1 gallon = 16 cups (or 4 quarts)
1 peck = 8 quarts
1 bushel = 4 pecks
1 pound = 454 grams

Fahrenheit	Celsius
250°–300°	121°–149°
300°–325°	149°–163°
325°–350°	163°–177°
375°	191°
400°–425°	204°–218°

FRENCH ONION CHICKEN

2 pounds boneless, skinless chicken breasts
1 (8 ounce) bottle French salad dressing
1 (2 ounce) envelope onion soup mix
1 (10 ounce) can whole cranberry sauce

Add all ingredients to slow cooker and stir to coat chicken. Cook on low for 8 hours. Serve with rice or pasta.

SPINACH BOW-TIE PASTA

1½ pounds lean ground beef,
browned with 1 medium onion and 1 clove minced garlic
1 (16 ounce) can tomato sauce
1 (14 ounce) can stewed tomatoes
1 teaspoon oregano
1 teaspoon Italian seasoning
Salt to taste
Pepper to taste
1 (10 ounce) package frozen chopped spinach, thawed
1 (16 ounce) package bow-tie pasta, cooked and drained
½ cup grated Parmesan cheese
1½ cups shredded mozzarella cheese

Combine all ingredients in slow cooker except spinach, pasta, and cheeses. Cook on high for 4 hours. Stir in spinach, cooked pasta, and cheeses during last ½ hour of cooking.

SODA POP CHICKEN

1 cup packed brown sugar
⅔ cup vinegar
¼ cup lemon-lime soda
2 to 3 tablespoons minced garlic
2 tablespoons soy sauce
1 teaspoon pepper
4 to 5 boneless, skinless chicken breasts

Combine all ingredients in slow cooker except chicken. Mix well. Add chicken and cook on low for 6 to 8 hours. Serve alone or over rice or noodles.

CHICKEN CACCIATORE

3 pounds boneless, skinless chicken breasts
¼ cup olive oil
2 teaspoons seasoned salt
1 (2 ounce) envelope spaghetti sauce mix
1 (16 ounce) can diced tomatoes
¼ cup white grape juice or apple juice
1 cup sliced mushrooms
1 green bell pepper, chopped

In large skillet, brown chicken in oil with seasoned salt. Place chicken in slow cooker. Combine remaining ingredients, except bell pepper, in skillet. Cook and stir until hot. Pour over chicken. Cook on low for 5 to 6 hours, adding bell pepper during last 20 minutes of cooking. Serve over spaghetti.

TASTY MEATBALLS

1 (2 ounce) envelope onion soup mix
3 cloves garlic, minced
1 (10 ounce) jar beef gravy
3 tablespoons water
$\frac{1}{8}$ teaspoon pepper
3 pounds frozen cooked meatballs

Combine all ingredients except meatballs in slow cooker and mix well.
Add meatballs and stir carefully. Cook on low for 4 to 5 hours. Serve
with noodles or rice.

PULLED PORK BURRITOS

2 pounds boneless pork loin roast
1 medium sweet onion, thinly sliced
2 cups barbecue sauce
¼ cup chunky salsa
2 tablespoons chili powder
3 teaspoons taco seasoning
8 to 10 flour tortillas
2 cups shredded lettuce
2 cups chopped tomatoes
2 cups shredded cheddar cheese
1 cup sour cream

Place pork roast in slow cooker and arrange onion on top. In separate bowl, mix together barbecue sauce, salsa, chili powder, and taco seasoning. Pour over pork. Cook on low for 8 to 10 hours. Shred pork and spoon mixture into tortillas along with shredded lettuce, chopped tomatoes, shredded cheese, and sour cream.

TAMALE CORN PIE

¼ cup yellow cornmeal
1½ cups milk
1 egg, beaten
1 pound lean ground beef, browned and drained
1 (2 ounce) envelope chili seasoning mix
1 tablespoon seasoned salt
1 (16 ounce) can diced tomatoes
1 (16 ounce) can corn, drained
1 (2 ounce) jar sliced black olives, drained
1 cup shredded cheddar cheese

Combine cornmeal, milk, and egg in slow cooker. Add remaining ingredients except cheese. Cook on high for 4 hours, adding cheese during last 10 minutes.

Less-expensive cuts of meat cook well
in slow cookers because they have less fat,
which makes them more suited to slow cooker recipes.
Long cooking times result in very moist and tender meats.

STUFFED PEPPERS

1½ pounds lean ground beef
1 egg
1 tablespoon Italian dressing
½ cup dried bread crumbs
¼ teaspoon salt
½ teaspoon garlic powder
¼ teaspoon pepper
¼ teaspoon crushed red pepper
1 cup instant rice (uncooked)
6 green bell peppers, tops removed and cleaned
1 (24 ounce) jar spaghetti sauce

Combine all ingredients except peppers and spaghetti sauce, and spoon into prepared peppers. Place in large slow cooker and add spaghetti sauce. Cook on high for 1 hour then on low for 7 hours. Top with grated Parmesan cheese if desired.

LEMON CHICKEN DINNER

Juice of 2 lemons
¼ teaspoon paprika
½ teaspoon celery salt
½ teaspoon salt
½ teaspoon pepper
1 (10 ounce) can cream of mushroom soup
1 (10 ounce) can cream of celery soup
4 boneless, skinless chicken breasts
4 to 6 small red potatoes
½ cup grated Parmesan cheese

Combine all ingredients in slow cooker except chicken, potatoes, and cheese. Mix well and add chicken. Top with potatoes. Cook on low for 8 hours. Sprinkle with cheese and serve.

CHILIES
& STEWS

"Give us today our daily bread."
MATTHEW 6:11 NIV

AUNTIE EM'S CHILI

1 (16 ounce) can tomato sauce
1 (15½ ounce) can kidney beans, drained
2 tablespoons chili powder
1 pound hamburger, browned

Combine all ingredients in slow cooker and cook on low at least 2 hours.

CORY'S WHITE CHILI

1 pound boneless, skinless chicken breasts,
cooked and cut into bite-size pieces
1 medium onion, chopped
1½ teaspoons garlic powder
2 (16 ounce) cans great northern beans, drained
1 (15 ounce) can chicken broth
1 teaspoon salt
1 teaspoon oregano
½ teaspoon pepper
¼ teaspoon red pepper
2 (4 ounce) cans diced green chilies
1 cup light sour cream
½ cup half-and-half

Add all ingredients to slow cooker except sour cream and half-and-half.
Cook on high for 3 to 4 hours. Add sour cream and half-and-half in last
hour of cooking. Serve hot.

Stir in dried spices during the last hour of cooking.
This will allow their flavors to be at their peak
when the dish is served. Use fresh herbs when possible.
These can be added first thing since they will hold
their flavor better when cooking for hours.

GREEK STEW

3 pounds stew beef, cubed
6 small onions, cut into wedges
3 cloves garlic, minced
1 (28 ounce) can tomatoes
½ cup beef stock
1 (6 ounce) can tomato paste
2 tablespoons red wine vinegar
2 teaspoons dried oregano

½ teaspoon salt
½ teaspoon pepper
½ cup flour
½ cup cold water
1 green bell pepper, chopped
Feta cheese
Fresh parsley

Combine beef, onion, garlic, tomatoes, beef stock, tomato paste, vinegar, oregano, salt, and pepper in slow cooker and cook on low for 8 hours. Mix together flour and cold water. Add to slow cooker along with green pepper. Cook on high for 15 minutes or until thickened. Serve sprinkled with feta cheese crumbles and fresh parsley.

HOT TOMATO STEW

2 pounds ground beef or cubed lean stew beef
1 (8 ounce) can tomato sauce
1 (6 ounce) can tomato paste
1 (16 ounce) can stewed tomatoes (optional)
2 tablespoons chili powder
1½ teaspoons salt
½ teaspoon hot pepper sauce

Combine all ingredients in slow cooker. Cover and cook on low for 8 to 10 hours.

MEXICAN CHILI

1 pound lean ground beef
2 (15½ ounce) cans red kidney beans, drained
1 (28 ounce) can diced tomatoes
¼ cup chopped celery
1 cup chopped onion
1 (6 ounce) can tomato paste
½ cup chopped green pepper
1 (4 ounce) can diced green chilies
2 tablespoons sugar
½ teaspoon garlic powder
1 teaspoon salt
1 teaspoon dried, crushed leaf marjoram
⅛ teaspoon pepper
1 bay leaf

Brown ground beef in skillet and drain. Add all ingredients to slow cooker. Cook on low for 8 to 10 hours. Remove bay leaf and stir before serving.

SOUTHWEST CHICKEN STEW

3 boneless, skinless chicken breasts
1 (15 ounce) can diced tomatoes with green chilies
1 (15 ounce) can black beans, undrained
2 (10½ ounce) cans cream of chicken soup
3 cups canned or frozen corn
2 cups chicken broth

Combine all ingredients in slow cooker. Cook on low for 8 hours. Remove chicken and shred or cut into chunks. Return to slow cooker and serve.

PINTO AND BLACK BEAN CHILI

1 cup chopped sweet onion
¼ teaspoon crushed red pepper flakes
1 teaspoon garlic salt
1 tablespoon chili powder
2 teaspoons ground cumin
1 teaspoon dried leaf oregano
1 (28 ounce) can diced tomatoes in juice
1 tablespoon soy sauce
1½ cups water
1 (6 ounce) can tomato paste
1 tablespoon red wine vinegar
2 (15 ounce) cans black beans, drained
2 (15 ounce) cans pinto beans, drained

Add all ingredients to slow cooker except black beans and pinto beans.
Stir well. Cook on low for 8 hours. Stir in beans 1 hour before serving.

AMAZING BEEF STEW

2 cups chopped carrots
3 cups chopped raw potatoes
2 small apples, chopped
2 pounds beef stew beef, cut into pieces
2 teaspoons salt
½ teaspoon thyme
2 tablespoons minced onion
2 cups apple cider
1 to 2 tablespoons flour

Place vegetables and apples in slow cooker.
Add meat and sprinkle with salt, thyme,
and onion. Add cider. Cook on low heat 10
to 12 hours. Thicken with flour during last
hour of cooking.

A slow cooker works best when it is two-thirds full.
More food may lead to an undercooked meal,
and less food may lead to an overcooked meal.

EASY CINCINNATI CHILI

2 pounds ground beef, browned
2 cups water
1 teaspoon allspice
1 teaspoon ground cloves
1 bay leaf
1 (6 ounce) can tomato paste
1 large onion, chopped
2 tablespoons chili powder
2 garlic cloves, minced
1½ teaspoons salt
1 teaspoon cinnamon
1 teaspoon nutmeg
1 teaspoon crushed red pepper
2 teaspoons unsweetened cocoa
2 teaspoons Worcestershire sauce
1 (15½ ounce) can kidney beans, drained

Add all ingredients to slow cooker except beans. Cook on low for 8 hours, adding beans 1 hour before serving. Remove bay leaf. Serve over hot spaghetti and top with chopped onions and shredded cheese.

MIGHTY MINESTRONE

3 cups water
2 pounds stew beef, cut into pieces
1 medium onion, diced
2 cups diced carrots
1 (15 ounce) can diced tomatoes
2 teaspoons salt
10 ounce package of frozen mixed vegetables
1 tablespoon basil
1 teaspoon oregano
½ cup dry vermicelli

Combine all ingredients in slow cooker and
cook on low for 10 to 12 hours.

JAKE'S PIRATE STEW

1 cup sliced sweet onion
1 pound lean ground beef
¼ cup long grain rice, uncooked
2 cups diced raw potatoes
½ cup diced celery
2 cups sliced carrots
1 (15½ ounce) can kidney beans, drained
1 teaspoon salt
Dash pepper
¼ teaspoon chili powder
¼ teaspoon Worcestershire sauce
1 cup tomato sauce
½ cup water

Cook onions and beef in skillet until browned. Layer all ingredients in slow cooker in order given. Cook on low for 6 hours.

SEAFOOD
SUPPERS

"You will have plenty to eat, until you are full, and you will praise the name of the Lord your God, who has worked wonders for you."

JOEL 2:26 NIV

LARRY'S LOBSTER DISH

1 (10 ounce) can cream of celery soup
5 ounces lobster (canned or frozen), flaked
¼ cup evaporated milk
½ cup fresh sliced mushrooms
2 egg yolks
2 tablespoons red wine vinegar

Combine all ingredients in slow cooker. Cook on low for 4 to 6 hours.

SHRIMP ALFREDO

1 onion, chopped
3 cloves garlic, minced
2 cups baby carrots
3 tablespoons milk
1 (16 ounce) jar alfredo sauce
½ teaspoon dried thyme leaves
½ teaspoon salt
⅛ teaspoon white pepper
½ teaspoon dried basil leaves
1 (10 ounce) package frozen cooked shrimp, thawed
2 cups frozen peas, thawed
½ cup grated Parmesan cheese

Place onion, garlic, and carrots in slow cooker. Mix milk, alfredo sauce, and spices. Add to slow cooker. Cook on low for 6 hours. Turn heat to high. Add shrimp and peas during last 20 minutes of cooking. Stir in cheese and serve over pasta.

BEAUTIFUL VEGGIES

Add tender vegetables such as fresh tomatoes, mushrooms, and zucchini during last 45 minutes of cooking time so they don't overcook.

CHEESY SALMON BAKE

1 (15 ounce) can salmon, undrained
1 (4 ounce) can mushrooms, drained
1½ cups bread crumbs
2 eggs
1 cup shredded cheddar cheese
1 tablespoon lemon juice
1 tablespoon minced onion

Combine all ingredients in lightly greased slow cooker. Cook on low for 3 to 5 hours.

SLOW-COOKER GUMBO

3 tablespoons flour
3 tablespoons olive oil
½ pound smoked sausage, sliced
2 cups frozen cut okra
1 green bell pepper, chopped
3 cloves garlic, minced
¼ teaspoon cayenne pepper
¼ teaspoon black pepper
1 (14 ounce) can diced tomatoes
1 (10 ounce) package frozen cooked shrimp, thawed

Combine flour and oil in small saucepan. Cook, stirring constantly, about 10 minutes until mixture starts to brown. Place flour mixture in slow cooker. Stir in all remaining ingredients except shrimp. Cook on low for 8 hours. Stir in shrimp during last 20 minutes of cooking. Serve over rice.

SHRIMP FIESTA

½ teaspoon oregano
2 cups water
½ teaspoon taco seasoning
1 cup instant rice
2 cloves garlic, minced
¼ cup butter
¼ cup pimento
1 (5 ounce) can albacore tuna
1 (10 ounce) package frozen cooked shrimp, thawed

Combine all ingredients in slow cooker except shrimp. Cook on low for 4 to 5 hours. Add shrimp during last 20 minutes of cooking.

JAMBALAYA

2 large onions, chopped
4 celery stalks, chopped
1 green bell pepper, chopped
1 clove garlic, minced
1 (16 ounce) can diced tomatoes
1 (16 ounce) can tomato sauce
1 teaspoon thyme
1 teaspoon basil
2 cups chicken broth
¼ teaspoon paprika
1 teaspoon salt
1 pound Italian sausage links, browned and sliced
2 pounds tilapia sprinkled with ¼ teaspoon each of pepper
and paprika and browned

Sauté onion, celery, green pepper, and garlic until limp. Add all ingredients to slow cooker and stir. Cook on low 3 hours or until done.

TUNA LINGUINE

2 (10 ounce) cans cream of celery soup
⅓ cup chicken broth
⅔ cup milk
1 tablespoon parsley
1 (10 ounce) package frozen peas, thawed
2 (7 ounce) cans albacore tuna, drained
1 (10 ounce) package linguine, cooked until just tender

In greased slow cooker, combine all ingredients except linguine. Cook on low for 6 hours, adding linguine during last hour of cooking.

SWEET AND SOUR SHRIMP

2 tablespoons cornstarch
3 tablespoons sugar
1 cup water
1 chicken bouillon cube
1 (13 ounce) can pineapple chunks, drained; (reserve juice)
2 teaspoons soy sauce
½ teaspoon ground ginger
1 (10 ounce) package frozen cooked shrimp, thawed
2 cups frozen peas
1 tablespoon vinegar

Combine cornstarch, sugar, and water in saucepan. Bring to boil and add bouillon, pineapple juice, soy sauce, and ginger. Cook for 1 minute. Add sauce and pineapple to slow cooker. Stir gently. Cook on low for 4 hours. Turn to high and add shrimp, peas, and vinegar. Stir and cook for 20 more minutes. Serve over rice.

NO PEEKING!

Avoid the temptation to lift the lid—
especially if you are cooking on the low setting.
Each time you lift the lid,
enough heat will escape that the cooking time
should be extended by 20 to 30.
To check progress without lifting the lid,
spin the cover until the condensation falls off.
Then it's easy to see inside.

CITRUS FISH

1 ½ pounds white fish fillets,
sprinkled with salt and pepper to taste and browned
½ cup chopped onion
4 tablespoons chopped fresh parsley
1 tablespoon olive oil
2 teaspoons grated lemon rind
2 teaspoons grated orange rind

Place fish in greased slow cooker.
Add onion, parsley, grated rind,
and oil. Cook on low for 3 hours
or until done.

SWISS CRAB CASSEROLE

¼ cup chopped celery
½ cup finely chopped onion
1 small green bell pepper, chopped
3 tablespoons butter
3 tablespoons flour
3 chicken bouillon cubes
2½ cups water
1 cup instant rice
2 (7 ounce) cans crabmeat, flaked
1 (4 ounce) can sliced mushrooms
1 cup butter crackers, crumbled
2½ cups shredded Swiss cheese, divided

Sauté vegetables in butter. Remove from heat and stir in flour. Dissolve bouillon cubes in boiling water. Add all ingredients to slow cooker except crackers and ½ cup shredded cheese. Stir. Cook on high for 4 hours. Top with crackers and remaining cheese.

SALMON CASSEROLE

3 (16 ounce) cans salmon
10 slices bread cut into 1-inch pieces
1 (15 ounce) can tomato sauce
1 green bell pepper, finely chopped
1 tablespoon lemon juice
1 (10 ounce) can condensed cream of onion soup
2 chicken bouillon cubes, crushed
6 eggs, well beaten
1 (10 ounce) can condensed cream of celery soup
½ cup milk

Combine all ingredients in greased slow cooker except cream of celery soup and milk. Cook on low for 4 to 5 hours. In saucepan, combine cream of celery soup with milk and heat. Serve over salmon.

VEGGIE CASSEROLES
& SIDES

"The joy of God is your strength!"
NEHEMIAH 8:10 MSG

GERMAN POTATO SALAD

3 cups potatoes, peeled and diced
½ cup chopped onions
½ cup sliced celery
¼ cup diced green bell pepper
¼ cup vinegar
¼ cup oil
1 teaspoon salt
⅛ teaspoon pepper
3 tablespoons sugar
4 to 6 slices bacon, cooked and crumbled

Combine all ingredients in slow cooker except bacon. Cook for 5 to 6 hours on low. Add bacon and garnish with fresh parsley.

SPINACH SOUFFLÉ

2 pounds frozen spinach, thawed and drained
¼ cup grated onion
1 (8 ounce) package light cream cheese, softened
½ cup mayonnaise
½ cup shredded cheddar cheese
2 eggs, beaten
¼ teaspoon salt
¼ teaspoon pepper
Dash nutmeg

Combine all ingredients in greased
slow cooker. Cook on high for
2 to 3 hours or until done.

WILD RICE ALMOND BAKE

2 cups wild rice, uncooked
1 cup slivered almonds
½ cup chopped sweet onions
¼ cup chopped celery
1 (8 ounce) can mushrooms, drained
6 cups vegetable broth
¼ teaspoon salt
⅛ teaspoon pepper
¼ teaspoon garlic salt
1 tablespoon parsley

Wash and drain rice. Combine all ingredients in slow cooker. Cook on low for 4 to 6 hours or until rice is done. Do not remove lid before rice has cooked 4 hours.

Slow-cooked dishes tend to lose their color.
Try using garnishes such as chopped fresh parsley, chives,
tomatoes, and red or green peppers
to add color to finished dishes.

SPICY MUSHROOMS & ONIONS

2 large sweet onions, thinly sliced
6 tablespoons butter
2 teaspoons basil
1 teaspoon oregano
1 teaspoon thyme
½ cup lemon juice
¼ teaspoon red pepper flakes
3 pounds whole mushrooms, cleaned

Sauté onion in butter. Add all ingredients to slow cooker except mushrooms. Cook on low for 1 hour.
Add mushrooms and stir carefully.
Cook for 30 more minutes and serve.

CREAMY VEGETABLE CASSEROLE

8 medium potatoes, peeled and cubed
1 sweet onion, diced
1 cup sliced carrots
½ cup sliced celery
4 chicken bouillon cubes
1 tablespoon parsley
5 cups water
⅓ cup butter
1 (13 ounce) can evaporated milk

Combine all ingredients in slow cooker except evaporated milk. Cover and cook 10 hours. Stir in evaporated milk during last hour of cooking.

RED BEANS AND RICE

2 (15 ounce) cans red beans
1 sweet onion, chopped
2 cups water
½ cup brown sugar
⅓ cup vinegar
½ cup salsa
1 cup instant rice

Combine all ingredients in slow cooker. Cook on low for 3 to 4 hours.

BACON RANCH POTATOES

2 (8 ounce) packages cream cheese
2 (2 ounce) envelopes ranch dressing mix
2 (10 ounce) cans cream of potato soup
½ cup bacon bits
2 (24 ounce) bags frozen hash browns, partially thawed

Combine all ingredients in slow cooker except hash browns. Add hash browns and stir well. Cook on low 7 to 9 hours. Stir before serving.

ACORN SQUASH

3 acorn squash, cut in half and seeded
2 teaspoons salt
$\frac{1}{2}$ teaspoon pepper
5 tablespoons butter
2 tablespoons brown sugar
$\frac{1}{2}$ cup water

Sprinkle squash with salt and pepper. Mix butter and brown sugar.
Fill squash with mixture. Pour water into slow cooker. Add squash
so they do not rest directly on top of each other. Cook on high for
1 hour. Reduce to low and cook for 5 to 6 more hours until done.

CLEANUP IN A SNAP

Always spray the slow cooker's crock with nonstick cooking spray or use a removable plastic liner for easy cleanup.

ITALIAN GREEN BEANS

1 (15 ounce) can diced tomatoes
4 (8 ounce) cans sliced mushrooms, undrained
½ teaspoon garlic powder
½ teaspoon oregano
3 (16 ounce) cans Italian cut green beans, 2 of them drained
½ cup Parmesan cheese

Combine all ingredients in slow cooker. Cook on low for 3 hours.

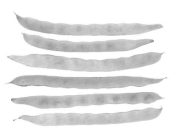

CREAMY NEW POTATOES

2 pounds small new potatoes, scrubbed and peeled
1 (10 ounce) can cream of mushroom soup
¼ cup sour cream
2 tablespoons water
2 tablespoons chopped green onions
1 medium garlic clove, minced
½ teaspoon dillweed
1 teaspoon salt

Place potatoes in slow cooker. Stir together remaining ingredients and pour over potatoes. Cover and cook on low 5 to 6 hours.

VEGGIE CASSEROLE

½ cup instant rice
1 pound sliced zucchini
1 pound sliced yellow squash
1 sweet onion, thinly sliced
1 green bell pepper, cut into strips
2 large tomatoes, thinly sliced
½ cup brown sugar
¼ cup olive oil

Spray slow cooker with nonstick cooking spray and add rice. Layer vegetables into cooker in order listed. Sprinkle brown sugar over vegetables and drizzle with olive oil. Cook for 6 hours on low.

DESSERTS & BEVERAGES

"When you call on me, when you come and pray to me, I'll listen."
JEREMIAH 29:12 MSG

PEACH COBBLER

⅓ cup sugar
½ cup brown sugar, packed
¼ cup biscuit mix
2 eggs
2 teaspoons vanilla
2 teaspoons butter, melted
¼ cup evaporated milk
2½ cups sliced frozen peaches, thawed
½ teaspoon cinnamon

Lightly butter slow cooker. Combine sugars and baking mix in cooker. Add eggs and vanilla. Stir to blend. Add butter and milk and stir. Mix in peaches and cinnamon. Cook on low for 6 to 8 hours. Serve warm with vanilla ice cream.

EASY CHERRY CHOCOLATE DESSERT

1 (21 ounce) can cherry pie filling
1 (18 ounce) package chocolate fudge cake mix
½ cup butter

Place pie filling in slow cooker. Combine dry cake mix and butter.
Sprinkle over filling. Cover and cook on low for 3 hours.

APPLE BUTTER

3 pounds Red Delicious apples, peeled and finely chopped
2 pounds Granny Smith apples, peeled and chopped
4 cups sugar
2 teaspoons cinnamon
¼ teaspoon ground cloves
¼ teaspoon salt

Place apples in slow cooker. In separate bowl, combine sugar, cinnamon, cloves, and salt. Pour over apples and mix well. Cook on high for 1 hour. Turn heat to low and cook for 9 to 11 hours or until dark brown and thick. Stir occasionally. Uncover and cook on low for 1 hour longer. Whisk until smooth. Serve or freeze.

KEEPING NUTS FRESH

To keep nuts fresh, double bag in tightly sealed
freezer bags and place in freezer.
Most nuts can be kept this way for up to 6 months.
When you are ready to prepare,
just pull from freezer and chop.

CHERRY COBBLER

2 (21 ounce) cans cherry pie filling
1 (18 ounce) package yellow cake mix
¼ cup butter, softened
Chopped pecans for garnish

Pour pie filling into slow cooker and spread evenly. In separate bowl, combine dry cake mix with butter until crumbly. Sprinkle cake mix over pie filling. Cook on low for 3 to 4 hours. Serve warm with vanilla ice cream and sprinkle with chopped pecans.

APPLESAUCE

1½ pounds Golden Delicious apples, peeled and sliced
⅓ cup sugar
½ teaspoon cinnamon
2 tablespoons lemon juice
¼ teaspoon nutmeg

Spread apple slices in slow cooker. Sprinkle with sugar and cinnamon. Add lemon juice. Cook on low for 6½ to 8 hours or until thick. Whisk until smooth. Sprinkle with nutmeg.

RICE PUDDING

1 ½ cups scalded milk
2½ cups cooked white rice
3 eggs, beaten
⅔ cup light brown sugar
1 teaspoon nutmeg
1 teaspoon cinnamon
1 teaspoon salt
2 tablespoons vanilla
3 tablespoons butter, softened

Combine all ingredients in lightly greased slow cooker. Cook on high for 1 to 2 hours, stirring occasionally.

BLUEBERRY DUMP CAKE

1 (21 ounce) can blueberry pie filling
1 box yellow cake mix
½ cup butter, softened
Vanilla ice cream

Place pie filling in slow cooker. Combine dry cake mix and butter until crumbly. Sprinkle over filling. Cook on low for 2 to 3 hours. Serve warm with vanilla ice cream.

WARM PINEAPPLE PUNCH

1 (46 ounce) can pineapple juice
3 cups orange juice, medium pulp
¼ cup fresh lemon juice
2 cinnamon sticks

Pour pineapple juice into slow cooker, followed by orange juice and lemon juice. Add cinnamon sticks. Cook on low for 2 hours. Remove cinnamon sticks. Serve warm. Garnish with oranges and fresh pineapple chunks.

TRIPLE CHOCOLATE DELIGHT

1 (18 ounce) package chocolate fudge cake mix
1 (16 ounce) carton sour cream
1 (4 ounce) package instant chocolate pudding
1 (12 ounce) bag milk chocolate chips
¼ cup oil
4 eggs
1 cup water

Spray slow cooker with nonstick cooking spray. Mix all ingredients. Pour into slow cooker. Cook on low for 4 to 5 hours.

CANNED FOOD MEASUREMENTS

The following chart will help you determine
the quantity in cups that a can of food holds.
A quick rule of thumb is 2 ounces
equals approximately ¼ cup.

Can Size	Approximate Measure
8 ounces	1 cup
10½ ounces	1¼ cups
12 ounces	1½ cups
14 ounces	1¾ cups
16 ounces	2 cups
20 ounces	2½ cups
29 ounces	3½ cups
43 ounces	4 cups

RAISIN RICE PUDDING

1 (16 ounce) carton half-and-half
3 eggs
⅔ cup sugar
2 teaspoons vanilla
1½ cups cooked rice
¼ cup raisins
½ teaspoon nutmeg

Lightly butter slow cooker. Whisk together half-and-half, eggs, sugar, and vanilla. Beat well. Pour into slow cooker. Stir in rice and raisins. Sprinkle nutmeg on top. Cook on high for 30 minutes. Stir well. Cook on low for 2 to 3 more hours.

CARAMEL MONKEY ROLLS

½ cup packed brown sugar
¼ cup pecans
2 (8 ounce) packages refrigerated, uncooked biscuits
¼ cup butter, melted
Cinnamon to taste
Sugar to taste

Mix brown sugar and pecans. Dip each uncooked biscuit in melted butter then into brown sugar and pecan mixture. Layer biscuits buttered slow cooker. Sprinkle cinnamon and sugar over each layer of biscuits. Cook on high 3 to 4 hours without lifting lid.

APPLE WALNUT DUMP CAKE

1 (21 ounce) can apple pie filling
½ cup butter
1 box yellow cake mix
½ cup chopped walnuts

Put pie filling into slow cooker. Cut butter into cake mix then sprinkle over pie filling. Sprinkle walnuts over top. Cook on low for 2 to 3 hours. Serve warm.

APPLE CIDER

12 cups apple juice
¼ cup brown sugar
½ teaspoon ground cloves
¼ teaspoon ground allspice
3 cinnamon sticks
1 orange, sliced

Combine all ingredients in slow cooker.
Cook on low for 2 to 3 hours, stirring
occasionally. Serve warm.

CRANBERRY PUNCH

3 cups cranberry juice cocktail
2 cups pineapple juice
½ cup water
½ cup sugar
½ teaspoon cinnamon
⅛ teaspoon ground cloves
⅛ teaspoon ground nutmeg

Combine all ingredients in slow cooker.
Cover and cook on low for 2 to 3 hours
until hot. Serve warm.

HONEY APPLE TEA

1 (12 ounce) can frozen apple juice concentrate
2 tablespoons instant tea
1 tablespoon honey
1 cinnamon stick

Prepare apple juice according to directions on label. Pour into slow cooker with remaining ingredients. Heat on low for 2 hours. Serve warm.

SPICY LEMONADE

4 cups cranberry juice cocktail
$\frac{1}{3}$ cup sugar
1 (12 ounce) can frozen lemonade concentrate, thawed
4 cups water
1 tablespoon honey
1 cinnamon stick
1 fresh lemon, sliced

Combine all ingredients in slow cooker. Cook on low for 2 to 3 hours.
Chill before serving.

SPICY TOMATO JUICE

10 large tomatoes, chopped into chunks
1 teaspoon salt
½ teaspoon seasoned salt
¼ teaspoon pepper
1 teaspoon sugar
¼ teaspoon chili powder

Combine all ingredients in slow cooker. Cook on low for 6 hours or until tomatoes are soft. Press through sieve. Chill and serve.

AVOID LINER CRACKS

A slow cooker liner can crack
if exposed to abrupt temperature shifts.
Don't put a hot ceramic liner directly on a cold countertop;
always set it on a dish towel or hot pad.
Likewise, don't put a chilled liner straight from
the refrigerator into a preheated base.

STRAWBERRY RHUBARB TOPPING

6 cups rhubarb, chopped
1 cup sugar
⅛ teaspoon cinnamon
½ cup white grape juice
2½ cups sliced strawberries

Combine all ingredients except strawberries in slow cooker. Cook on low for 6 hours or until rhubarb is tender. Add strawberries during last hour of cooking. Serve over shortcake.

PINEAPPLE DESSERT

1 cup white sugar
½ cup brown sugar
3 eggs
¼ cup butter, melted
¼ cup milk
1 (8 ounce) can crushed pineapple, drained
8 slices of white bread, crusts removed and cut into cubes

Combine all ingredients in slow cooker. Cook on high for 2 hours then on low for 1 hour. Serve with ice cream.

TAPIOCA DELIGHT

10 tablespoons large pearl tapioca
½ cup sugar
⅛ teaspoon salt
4 cups water
1 cup green grapes, halved
1 cup crushed pineapple
1 cup nondairy whipped topping
1 sliced banana
½ cup mandarin oranges, drained

Mix tapioca, sugar, salt, and water in slow cooker. Cook on high for 3 hours. Cool completely. Stir in remaining ingredients and serve cold.

PUMPKIN PUDDING

1 (15 ounce) can pumpkin puree
1 tablespoon pumpkin pie spice
2 teaspoons vanilla
1 (12 ounce) can evaporated milk
½ cup white sugar
¼ cup brown sugar
½ cup biscuit baking mix
2 tablespoons butter
2 eggs

Spray slow cooker with nonstick cooking spray. Beat all ingredients until smooth in mixing bowl and add to slow cooker. Cook on low 6 to 8 hours. Serve with whipped topping.

POMEGRANATE PUNCH

3 cups pomegranate juice
1 cup cranberry juice cocktail
½ cup orange juice
⅛ teaspoon cinnamon
½ teaspoon ginger

Combine all ingredients in slow cooker. Stir well. Cook on low for 2 to 3 hours until hot.

COMFORT IN A MUG

¼ cup brown sugar
4 cups water
¼ teaspoon salt
¼ teaspoon nutmeg
¼ teaspoon cinnamon
¼ teaspoon allspice
½ teaspoon ground cloves
2 (16 ounce) cans jellied cranberry sauce
2 cups pineapple juice
1 tablespoon butter

Combine all ingredients in slow cooker except butter. Stir well. Cook on low for 3 to 4 hours. Add butter just before serving.

FRUIT PUNCH

8 cups water
1 (12 ounce) can frozen cranberry-raspberry juice concentrate, thawed
1 (12 ounce) can frozen lemonade concentrate, thawed
¼ cup sugar
¼ teaspoon cinnamon

Combine all ingredients in slow cooker. Cook on low for 4 hours or until heated through. Chill.

MEXICAN SPINACH

3 (10 ounce) packages frozen chopped spinach, thawed
1 sweet onion, chopped
1 clove garlic, minced
1 tablespoon canola oil
2 green chilies, toasted, peeled, and minced
3 fresh tomatillos, chopped

In large skillet over medium heat, cook onion and garlic in oil for about 5 minutes. Add chilies and tomatillos. Cook for 2 more minutes. Add mixture and spinach to slow cooker. Cook on low 4 to 6 hours. Stir and serve topped with sour cream.

ITALIAN VEGETABLE CASSEROLE

1 large onion, thinly sliced
2 medium zucchini, sliced
2 cups fresh mushrooms, sliced
1 tablespoon olive oil
1 teaspoon salt
4 Roma tomatoes, sliced
2 cups shredded mozzarella cheese
2 cups tomato sauce
1 teaspoon oregano
Salt and pepper to taste

In large skillet, sauté onion, zucchini, and mushrooms in oil until slightly tender. Add salt and mix well. In slow cooker, layer of vegetables, of tomato sauce, and of cheese. Sprinkle with oregano, salt, and pepper. Repeat layers twice. Cook on low for 6 to 8 hours.

EASY VEGGIE TRIO

3 cups sliced potatoes
3 cups sliced carrots
½ cup chopped sweet onions
1 (15 ounce) can beef broth
1 teaspoon salt

Combine all ingredients in slow cooker. Cook on high for 4 to 6 hours.

CHEESY VEGETABLE CASSEROLE

1 (16 ounce) jar cheddar cheese pasta sauce
1 (8 ounce) package cream cheese
¼ cup hot water
¼ teaspoon pepper
3 (16 ounce) bags frozen California vegetables;
(broccoli, cauliflower, and carrots)
½ cup milk
½ cup toasted sliced almonds

Combine in slow cooker cheese sauce, cream cheese, and hot water. Stir until smooth. Stir in pepper and frozen vegetables. Cook on low for 6 to 7 hours or until vegetables are tender. Add milk during last hour of cooking. Sprinkle with toasted almonds just before serving.

BROCCOLI RICE CASSEROLE

1 (10 ounce) can condensed cream of mushroom soup
1 (8 ounce) jar processed cheese sauce
1 cup milk
1 cup instant rice
1 small onion, chopped
1 teaspoon garlic salt
1 (16 ounce) package frozen broccoli cuts, thawed and drained

Combine in slow cooker soup, cheese sauce, milk, rice, onion, and garlic salt. Add broccoli and mix well. Cover and cook on low for 4 to 5 hours.

VEGETABLE MEDLEY

1 small green bell pepper
½ cup chopped celery
2 cups sliced carrots
1 small onion, sliced
2 cups frozen green beans, thawed
2 large tomatoes, chopped
4 tablespoons butter
1 tablespoon sugar
2½ teaspoons salt
¼ teaspoon pepper
3 tablespoons tapioca

Combine all ingredients in slow cooker. Cook on high for 3 to 4 hours.

FOOD STORAGE

Remove cooked food from
the slow cooker before refrigeration.
Liners are made of very thick material
and do not cool quickly,
so if food is left in the slow cooker for storage,
it won't cool down quickly enough
to prevent the growth of bacteria.

CHEESY CREAMED CORN

3 (16 ounce) packages frozen corn
11 ounces package cream cheese
4 tablespoons butter
3 tablespoons water
3 tablespoons milk
2 tablespoons sugar
1 (10 ounce) can cheese sauce

Combine all ingredients in slow cooker. Cook for 4 to 5 hours on low.

CREAMY SUCCOTASH

1 cup dry lima beans, rinsed and drained
1 (16 ounce) package frozen corn
1 cup coarsely chopped red bell pepper
½ cup chopped sweet onion
¼ cup chopped celery
2 cloves garlic, minced
¼ teaspoon pepper
1 bay leaf
1 (10 ounce) can condensed cream of celery soup
1 cup water
6 slices bacon, cooked and crumbled

Combine in slow cooker beans, corn, pepper, onion, celery, garlic, pepper, and bay leaf. In separate bowl, combine soup and water. Add to slow cooker. Cook on low for 8 to 10 hours. Discard bay leaf and stir in bacon a few minutes before serving.

MACARONI AND CHEESE

1 (16 ounce) package macaroni, cooked and drained
½ pound processed American cheese
1 (10 ounce) can condensed cheese soup
1 cup butter
1 teaspoon salt
2 cups milk

Combine all ingredients in slow cooker. Cook on low for 1 hour, stir.

CHEESE SOUFFLÉ

8 slices white bread, with crusts removed, cut into fourths
2 cups shredded cheddar cheese
4 eggs
1 cup milk
1 cup evaporated milk
¼ teaspoon salt
1 tablespoon parsley
½ teaspoon paprika

Lightly grease slow cooker. Alternate layers of bread and cheese in slow cooker. Beat eggs with milk, evaporated milk, salt, parsley, and paprika. Pour egg mixture over top of bread and cheese. Cover and cook on low for 3 to 4 hours.

RICE PILAF

3 cups water
1½ cups instant brown rice
1 teaspoon salt
¼ cup chopped onion
¼ cup sliced carrots
1 cup beef broth
1 (4 ounce) can mushrooms
2 tablespoons parsley
¼ teaspoon marjoram
¼ teaspoon thyme

Combine all ingredients in slow cooker. Cook on low for 6 hours.

CHEESY POTATOES

1 (10 ounce) can condensed cream of mushroom soup
1 (8 ounce) carton sour cream
1½ cups shredded sharp cheddar cheese
1 (32 ounce) package frozen hash browns

Spray slow cooker with nonstick cooking spray. Combine soup, sour cream, and cheese in medium bowl and mix well. Pour half of potatoes into prepared slow cooker. Top with half of sour cream mixture. Add remaining potatoes and top with sour cream mixture, spreading evenly over all. Cook on high for 4 hours.

CANDIED CARROTS

3 cups baby carrots
⅓ cup dijon mustard
½ cup brown sugar
¼ teaspoon ginger
⅛ teaspoon pepper
½ teaspoon salt

Combine all ingredients in slow cooker. Cook on high for 2 to 3 hours or until carrots are tender, stirring occasionally.

TUNA STUFFED PEPPERS

1 (28 ounce) jar marinara sauce, divided
14 ounces canned tuna, drained and rinsed
1 teaspoon garlic salt
1 sweet onion, diced
½ cup butter cracker crumbs
4 green bell peppers

Leaving about ¼ cup of marinara sauce in jar, mix all ingredients together except bell peppers. Cut tops off peppers. Clean and hollow out. Put mixture in peppers and place in slow cooker. Cover with remaining ¼ cup of sauce. Cook on low heat for 9 hours.

SCALLOPED POTATOES AND SALMON

5 medium red potatoes, sliced and divided
3 tablespoons flour, divided
Salt to taste
Pepper to taste
1 (16 ounce) can salmon, drained and flaked
½ cup chopped onion
1 (10 ounce) can cream of mushroom soup
¼ cup water
⅛ teaspoon nutmeg

Place half of potatoes in well-buttered slow cooker. Sprinkle with half of flour, salt and pepper to taste, and half of salmon. Repeat layers once. Combine onion, soup, and water and pour into cooker. Top with nutmeg. Cover and cook on low for 7 to 9 hours or until potatoes are tender.

TUNA NOODLE CASSEROLE

2 (10 ounce) cans cream of mushroom soup
1/3 cup chicken broth
2/3 cup milk
2 tablespoons parsley flakes
1 (10 ounce) package frozen peas, thawed
2 (7 ounce) cans tuna, well drained
10 ounces medium egg noodles, cooked until just tender
3 tablespoons potato chip crumbs

Combine soup, chicken broth, milk, parsley, peas, and tuna in well-greased
slow cooker. Fold in cooked noodles. Top with potato chip crumbs.
Cover and cook on low for 5 to 6 hours.

CHEESY SHRIMP PASTA

2 pounds processed American cheese, cubed
16 ounces half-and-half
1 (10 ounce) can tomatoes with green chilies
1 small onion, chopped
1 clove garlic, minced
1 (10 ounce) package frozen cooked shrimp, thawed

Combine all ingredients in slow cooker except shrimp. Cook on low for 4 hours. Add shrimp and cook for 20 more minutes on high. Serve with pasta.

POACHED SALMON STEAKS

4 (7 ounce) salmon steaks
2 cups water
1 cup white grape juice
1 teaspoon salt
2 bay leaves
2 peppercorns
1 sprig fresh rosemary
1/2 teaspoon oregano
1 onion slice
1 sprig fresh parsley

Place salmon steaks in bottom of greased slow cooker. Add remaining ingredients to saucepan and heat until boiling. Pour over salmon and cook on low for approximately 3 hours. Remove bay leaves. Serve hot or cold with a salad.

Converted long-grain rice is the only type that can be prepared in a slow cooker. Other types of rice, such as brown, basmati, or jasmine, should be cooked separately and then added near the end of the slow cooker's cooking time.

TILAPIA

Salt to taste
Pepper to taste
1 tablespoon flour
2 (10 ounce) pieces of tilapia
4 tablespoons olive oil
1 large onion, finely chopped
1 (15 ounce) can diced tomatoes
1 tablespoon tomato puree
1 cup water
$\frac{1}{8}$ teaspoon red pepper

Add salt and pepper to flour and coat each piece of fish. In saucepan, slightly brown both sides of fish in olive oil and put into slow cooker. Sauté onion in same pan. Mix in tomatoes, tomato puree, and water. Bring to a boil and add red pepper. Pour over fish and cook on low for 4 to 6 hours. Serve with rice.

TUNA BAKE

1 (16 ounce) can white beans
1 (15 ounce) can diced tomatoes
2 (6 ounce) cans white tuna, drained and flaked
1½ teaspoons basil
1 teaspoon garlic salt
Salt to taste
Pepper to taste

Combine all ingredients in slow cooker. Cook on low for 3 to 4 hours.

SHRIMP MARINARA

1 (15 ounce) can diced tomatoes and onions
2 tablespoons fresh parsley, minced
1 clove of garlic, minced
¼ teaspoon seasoned salt
¼ teaspoon basil
1 teaspoon salt
½ teaspoon pepper
1 teaspoon oregano
1 (6 ounce) can tomato paste
1 (10 ounce) package frozen cooked shrimp, thawed

Combine all ingredients in slow cooker except shrimp. Cook on low for 6 hours. Turn control to high, stir in cooked shrimp, and continue cooking for 15 to 20 more minutes. Serve with spaghetti and Parmesan cheese.

CASHEW TUNA

1 (7 ounce) can tuna, drained
½ cup celery, diced
½ cup red onion, diced
3 tablespoons margarine
1 (10 ounce) can cream of mushroom soup
1 (16 ounce) can bean sprouts, drained
1 tablespoon soy sauce
1 cup cashews, chopped

Combine all ingredients in slow cooker. Stir well. Cover and cook on low setting for 6 to 8 hours. Serve with chow mein noodles.

SHRIMP CREOLE

½ cup diced celery
1 small onion, chopped
1 (8 ounce) can tomato sauce
1 (28 ounce) can whole tomatoes
1 teaspoon garlic salt
1 teaspoon salt
¼ teaspoon pepper
1 teaspoon Tabasco sauce
1 (10 ounce) package of frozen cooked shrimp, thawed
1 green bell pepper, chopped

Combine all ingredients in slow cooker except shrimp and bell pepper. Cook 4 hours on high or 8 hours on low. Add shrimp and bell pepper during last 20 minutes of cooking. Serve over rice.

PARSLEY FISH

1 ½ pounds white fish fillets, sprinkled with salt and pepper to taste
1 medium onion, chopped
5 tablespoons chopped parsley
4 teaspoons oil

Butter slow cooker and add all ingredients. Cook on low for 2 hours or until fish is done. Serve with white rice.

CHEESY CITRUS FISH

6 tablespoons butter
3 tablespoons flour
1 ½ teaspoons salt
1 teaspoon dry mustard
¼ teaspoon nutmeg
1 ¼ cups milk
1 teaspoon lemon juice
1 cup shredded cheddar cheese
3 pounds frozen white fish fillets, thawed

Over medium heat, melt butter in saucepan. Stir in flour, salt, mustard, and nutmeg. Add milk, stirring constantly until thickened. Add lemon juice and cheese. Stir until cheese is melted. Place fish in slow cooker and add sauce. Cook on high for 1 hour or until fish is flaky. Serve with rice.

TAHNEE'S TUNA CASSEROLE

2 (5 ounce) cans tuna, drained
1 (10 ounce) can cream of celery soup
3 hard-boiled eggs, chopped
½ cup diced celery
½ cup mayonnaise
¼ teaspoon pepper
1 cup crushed potato chips

Spray slow cooker with nonstick cooking spray. Combine all ingredients in slow cooker. Cook on low for 6 hours.

TACO CHILI

2 pounds lean ground beef
½ cup chopped onion
1 envelope taco seasoning mix
2 (15 ounce) cans diced tomatoes
1 (10 ounce) can diced tomatoes with green chilies
1 (16 ounce) can pinto beans, drained
1 (15 ounce) can chili beans in sauce
1 cup frozen corn

Brown beef and onion in large skillet. Drain and place in slow cooker along with remaining ingredients. Cook on low for 8 to 10 hours or on high for 4 to 5 hours. Top each serving with shredded cheese and crushed tortilla chips if desired.

SAUSAGE AND CHICKEN CHILI

2 boneless chicken breast halves, cooked and diced
12 ounces turkey sausage, cooked and crumbled
1 cup chopped sweet onion, sautéed
4 cloves garlic, minced
1½ cups salsa
1 cup chicken broth
1 (15 ounce) can diced tomatoes with juice
1 cup frozen corn
2 tablespoons finely chopped chili peppers
1½ teaspoons ground cumin
½ teaspoon salt
¼ teaspoon pepper
2 (16 ounce) cans great northern beans, drained
Fresh cilantro for garnish

Add all ingredients to slow cooker except beans and cilantro. Cover and cook on high for 4 hours. Add beans 1 hour before serving. Garnish with fresh cilantro.

CHICKEN STEW

3 chicken breasts, cooked and chopped
2 (28 ounce) cans whole tomatoes, diced
2 (6 ounce) cans tomato sauce
3 cups chopped carrots
3 cups chopped potatoes
2 cups frozen corn
2 basil leaves
½ cup minced sweet onions

Combine all ingredients in slow cooker. Cook on low for 6 to 8 hours.
Serve over rice.

BACON AND POTATO STEW

1 sweet onion, chopped
1 cup diced carrots
1 cup chopped cabbage
¼ cup chopped fresh parsley
4 cups beef broth
1 bay leaf
3 cups diced potatoes
2 teaspoons black pepper
1 teaspoon salt
¼ teaspoon nutmeg
½ cup sour cream
1 pound bacon, cooked and crumbled

Combine all ingredients except sour cream and bacon. Cook on low for 8 to 10 hours. Remove bay leaf. Remove potatoes with slotted spoon. Mash potatoes and mix with sour cream. Return to slow cooker and add bacon. Mix thoroughly and serve.

SIX CAN CHILI

¼ cup cornmeal
1 teaspoon chili powder
1 teaspoon paprika
½ cup prepared barbecue sauce
1 (28 ounce) can diced tomatoes
2 (15 ounce) cans chili without beans
1 (15 ounce) can pinto beans, undrained
1 (15 ounce) can chili beans, undrained
1 (10 ounce) can condensed French onion soup

Combine all ingredients in slow cooker. Cook on high 2 to 4 hours.

NAVY BEAN SOUP

8 ounces dried navy beans
1 (16 ounce) can stewed tomatoes
1 cup chopped carrots
1 cup frozen corn
1 (2 ounce) envelope onion soup mix
1 cup sliced okra
1 small sweet onion, sliced
1 tablespoon salt
Dash pepper
1 teaspoon sugar
1 tablespoon parsley
6 cups water

Rinse dried beans with hot water in strainer. Put beans in slow cooker; add remaining ingredients. Cook on high for 8 hours.

BEEF AND GREEN BEAN STEW

2 cups carrots, sliced
2 pounds stew beef, cut into pieces
2 teaspoons salt
3 cups potatoes, chopped
2 (6 ounce) cans green beans, drained
1 cup frozen corn
½ cup minced onions
2 (2 ounce) envelopes onion soup mix
3 cups water

Combine all ingredients in slow
cooker. Cook on high for 1 hour
then on low for 5 to 6 hours or until
carrots and beef are tender.

Potatoes, parsnips, turnips, and carrots
cook more slowly than meats in slow cooker.
Cutting them into cubes 1 inch or smaller
and placing them under the meat will ensure
that they get cooked thoroughly.

BEEF & GREEN CHILI STEW

1 pound stew beef, cut into pieces
1 tablespoon flour
1 tablespoon butter
1 onion, chopped
2 cloves garlic, minced
4 mild green chili peppers, seeded, chopped
½ teaspoon oregano
½ teaspoon ground cumin
½ cup beef broth

Dust beef with flour. Brown beef in butter with onion and garlic in skillet. Combine mixture in slow cooker with remaining ingredients. Cook on low 6 to 8 hours. Garnish with fresh chopped cilantro and serve with warm tortillas.

CORN CHOWDER

2 cups diced red potatoes
½ cup chopped onions
6 slices of bacon, cooked and diced (reserve drippings)
2 (10 ounce) packages frozen corn
1 (16 ounce) can cream-style corn
1 tablespoon sugar
1 teaspoon Worcestershire sauce
1 teaspoon seasoned salt
¼ teaspoon pepper
1 cup water

Sauté potatoes with chopped onions in bacon drippings. Combine all ingredients in slow cooker. Cook on low for 6 to 7 hours.

BEEF & MUSHROOM STEW

1½ pounds stew beef, cut into pieces
1 (10 ounce) can condensed French onion soup
½ cup red cooking wine
1 teaspoon salt
Dash pepper
Dash rosemary
2 cups potatoes, cubed
1 carrot, sliced
1 cup sliced fresh mushrooms
1 bay leaf
1 (16 ounce) can diced tomatoes
3 tablespoons flour mixed with just enough cold water to
make a smooth paste

Combine all ingredients except tomatoes and flour paste. Cover and cook on low for 8 to 10 hours. Add tomatoes 1 hour before done. Remove bay leaf. Thicken mixture with flour paste about 20 minutes before serving.

BLACK-EYED PEA & BEEF STEW

1 (16 ounce) package dried black-eyed peas, rinsed and drained
1 (10 ounce) can condensed bean and bacon soup
4 cups water
6 carrots, peeled and chopped
2 pounds stew beef, cut into pieces
¼ teaspoon pepper
¼ teaspoon salt

Combine all ingredients in slow cooker.
Cook on low for 9 to 10 hours
or until peas and beef are tender.

GROUND BEEF SOUP

1 pound ground beef, browned
¼ teaspoon pepper
¼ teaspoon oregano
¼ teaspoon basil
¼ teaspoon salt
¼ of 2-ounce envelope onion soup mix
3 cups boiling water
1 (8 ounce) can tomato sauce
2 tablespoons soy sauce
½ cup sliced celery
1 cup sliced carrots
1 cup elbow macaroni, cooked and drained
¼ cup grated Parmesan cheese

Combine all ingredients in slow cooker except macaroni and Parmesan cheese. Cook on low heat 6 to 8 hours. Turn to high heat and add macaroni and Parmesan cheese. Cook for 15 more minutes and serve.

ITALIAN CHICKEN STEW

4 raw boneless, skinless chicken breasts cut into chunks
1 onion, chopped
1 (15 ounce) can garbanzo beans, drained
1 (20 ounce) jar marinara sauce
1 teaspoon Italian seasoning
⅛ teaspoon pepper
1 green bell pepper, cut into chunks

Combine all ingredients except bell pepper in slow cooker. Cook on low for 6 to 7 hours, adding bell pepper during last hour of cooking.

SALSA CHICKEN

4 boneless chicken breasts
1 (28 ounce) can enchilada sauce
3 (16 ounce) jars tomato salsa

Combine all ingredients in slow cooker. Cook on high for 5 to 6 hours. Shred chicken and serve with rice and tortillas.

WILD WEST CASSEROLE

1 onion, chopped
1½ pounds ground beef, browned and drained
4 to 6 medium potatoes, sliced
1 (15½ ounce) can kidney beans
1 (10 ounce) can condensed tomato soup
½ teaspoon salt
½ teaspoon pepper
¼ teaspoon garlic salt

Put chopped onion in bottom of slow cooker. Add beef, potatoes, and beans. Spread soup over all. Do not stir. Sprinkle with seasonings. Cook on low for 8 hours.

RIGATONI PIZZA

1½ pounds hamburger, browned and drained
8 ounces rigatoni, cooked
1 pound pepperoni
1 cup sliced mushrooms
2 cups shredded mozzarella cheese
1 onion, diced
1 (10 ounce) can mushroom soup
1 (16 ounce) can spaghetti sauce

Layer all ingredients in slow cooker and cook on high for 2 to 3 hours.

HERB PORK ROAST

1 teaspoon garlic, minced
1 teaspoon salt
1 teaspoon ground thyme
½ teaspoon sage
½ teaspoon ground cloves
1 teaspoon grated lemon rind
5 pounds boneless pork roast
½ cup water
4 to 6 small red potatoes

Combine all spices and rub mixture into roast. Add water to slow cooker then add roast and potatoes. Cook on low for 9 to 10 hours until meat is tender and potatoes are done.

SWISS STEAK

2 (2 ounce) envelopes onion soup mix
1 soup can full of water
2 (10 ounce) cans of cream of mushroom soup
3 pounds round steak, trimmed and cut into serving sizes

Mix dry onion soup mix, water, and mushroom soup in slow cooker. Add steak and spoon mixture on top of steak. Cook on low for 8 hours. Serve with mashed potatoes or rice.

SWEET AND SOUR PORK

3 tablespoons soy sauce
2 tablespoons cornstarch
2 tablespoons water
¼ cup brown sugar
2 to 3 pounds cubed pork
3 cloves garlic, minced
¼ cup cider vinegar
1 sweet large onion, sliced
2 green bell peppers, cored and cut into quarters
2 cups pineapple chunks

Spray slow cooker with nonstick cooking spray. Combine soy sauce, cornstarch, water, and brown sugar in slow cooker. Mix well and add pork. Stir in remaining ingredients except green peppers and pineapple. Cook on low for 8 hours. Stir in peppers and pineapple during last 20 minutes of cooking. Serve with rice.

BEEF STROGANOFF

1 cup water
2 (6 ounce) cans mushrooms
1 (2 ounce) envelope onion soup mix
2 pounds stew beef, cut into bite-size pieces
1 tablespoon flour
1 cup sour cream

Combine water, mushrooms, and soup mix in slow cooker. Add beef and mix. Cook on high for 5 to 6 hours. In separate bowl, combine flour and sour cream. Add to slow cooker and cook ½ hour longer. Serve over hot cooked noodles.

Browning meat before putting it in the slow cooker helps to break down natural sugars and release fat-soluble food components, which enhances flavor. Sautéing vegetables with fresh herbs and whole spices before putting them in the slow cooker can also improve the flavor.

STEAK AND VEGETABLES

1 pound round steak, cut in serving pieces
1/8 teaspoon pepper
1 teaspoon salt
1/8 teaspoon garlic powder
1 (16 ounce) can diced tomatoes
2 cups of baby carrots
2 potatoes, scrubbed and cut in quarters
1 medium onion, peeled and quartered
1 green bell pepper, seeded and cut in quarters

Combine all ingredients in slow cooker except green pepper. Cook on low for 7 to 8 hours or until meat is tender. Add green pepper during last hour of cooking.

EASY BARBECUE RIBS

3 pounds ribs
Salt to taste
Pepper to taste
1 teaspoon garlic powder
2 cups bottled barbecue sauce

Broil ribs in broiler pan until well browned, turning occasionally. Remove fat, sprinkle ribs with salt and pepper, and cut into serving sizes. Put in slow cooker. Mix garlic powder with barbecue sauce and pour over ribs. Cover and cook on low for 6 to 8 hours or until tender. Serve with coleslaw and french fries.

PEACHY PORK CHOPS

Salt to taste
Pepper to taste
6 pork chops
1 (29 ounce) can peach halves (reserving ¼ cup syrup)
¼ cup brown sugar
¼ teaspoon ground cloves
1 (8 ounce) can tomato sauce
¼ cup vinegar

Salt and pepper each pork chop and brown lightly on both sides in skillet. Drain and place in slow cooker. Top with drained peaches. In separate bowl, combine brown sugar, cloves, tomato sauce, vinegar, and ¼ cup syrup from peaches. Pour tomato mixture over all. Cook on low for 6 to 8 hours or until chops are tender. Serve over mashed potatoes or rice.

CHICKEN CREOLE

3 pounds boneless, skinless chicken pieces
1 medium onion, chopped
¼ cup chopped celery
1 teaspoon salt
1 teaspoon thyme
½ teaspoon paprika
2 teaspoons parsley
1 (6 ounce) can diced tomatoes
1 (4 ounce) can mushrooms
1 green bell pepper, cut in strips

Combine all ingredients in slow cooker except bell pepper. Cook on high for 4 to 5 hours or until chicken is done. Add bell pepper during last hour of cooking.

CHICKEN MERLOT WITH MUSHROOMS

3 cups fresh mushrooms, sliced
1 large onion, chopped
2 cloves garlic, minced
3 pounds boneless, skinless chicken breast, cut into bite-size pieces
1 cup chicken broth
1 (6 ounce) can tomato paste
2 tablespoons quick-cooking tapioca
2 tablespoons basil
2 teaspoons sugar
¼ teaspoon salt
¼ teaspoon pepper

Place mushrooms, onion, and garlic in slow cooker. Top with chicken.
In separate bowl, combine remaining ingredients and pour over chicken.
Cook on low for 7 to 8 hours or until chicken is done. Serve with pasta.
Top with Parmesan cheese.

TERIYAKI STEAK

1 teaspoon ground ginger
1 tablespoon sugar
2 tablespoons olive oil
½ cup soy sauce
1 clove garlic, crushed
2 pounds boneless chuck steak, cut into ⅛-inch slices

Combine all ingredients except steak in slow cooker. Add steak.
Cook on low for 8 hours or until meat is tender. Serve with rice.

© 2010 by Barbour Publishing, Inc.

Compiled by MariLee Parrish.

ISBN 978-1-60260-742-2

Scripture quotations marked NIV are taken from the HOLY BIBLE, NEW INTERNATIONAL VERSION®. NIV®. Copyright © 1973, 1978, 1984 by International Bible Society. Used by permission of Zondervan. All rights reserved.

Scripture quotations marked MSG are from *THE MESSAGE*. Copyright © by Eugene H. Peterson 1993, 1994, 1995, 1996, 2000, 2001, 2002. Used by permission of NavPress Publishing Group.

Published by Barbour Publishing, Inc., P.O. Box 719, Uhrichsville, Ohio 44683, www.barbourbooks.com

Our mission is to publish and distribute inspirational products offering exceptional value and biblical encouragement to the masses.

 Member of the
Evangelical Christian
Publishers Association

Printed in China.